mxJC
4/2022

GAME ON!

DOMINOES
FOR BEGINNERS

JON TREMAINE

WINDMILL
BOOKS ™

INTRODUCTION

Dominoes originated in China over 2,000 years ago and the game has changed very little since then. Traditionally a domino is a slab of bone, wood, or plastic. It is twice as long as it is wide and is divided in half by a line down its center. Each half tile is either blank or contains a number of indented bold spots ranging from one to six.

Dominoes can be played on any flat surface, from your kitchen table to your bedroom floor!

The set of dominoes shown here is the most commonly used. It is called a "Double-6" set because the highest tile in the set is a double-six. There are 28 tiles in total.

THE LANGUAGE OF DOMINOES

Most games have their own language – words and phrases that are unique to the game. Dominoes is no exception. The domino tiles are placed with the **PIPS** (the spots) facedown on the center of the table. They are **SHUFFLED** (moved around so that no one knows where any particular tile is located). Players start by picking up the same number of tiles each. This is called **DRAWING YOUR HAND.** The dominoes left on the table after the draw has been made are called **THE BONEYARD.** This is the pool from which more tiles can be drawn depending upon the rules of the particular game.

In most domino games you have to **BUTT** one domino to another so that the pips match. For example, if your opponent has played a 5–3 tile, you can play any of your tiles that also have a 5 or a 3. Here are a few examples:

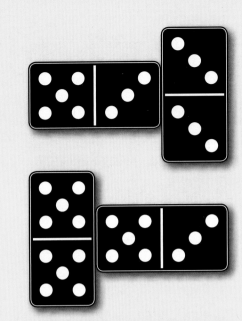

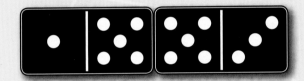

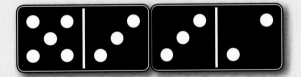

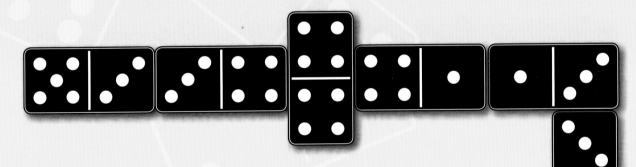

You have started the LINE OF PLAY. This line can be extended at either end.

Note that a double number is usually placed across the line of play. You can turn corners to suit the playing area.

GAME 1: BLOCK

This is the most popular game in North America. It can be played with individuals competing against each other but it is best played with four players who play in two teams. Your partner sits opposite you.

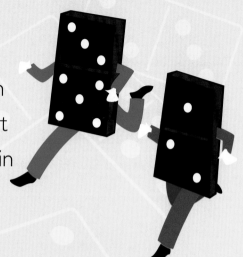

HOW TO PLAY

The dominoes are all placed **PIPS DOWN** on the table and all four players help to shuffle them. The players decide whether to start with five, six, or seven tiles. Each player now draws their hand, shielding the dominoes from their opponents by standing them on their long edges with the pips facing them.

The player who has drawn the double-six starts the game by placing it **PIPS UP** on the playing surface. If nobody has the double-six, then the highest double that has been drawn starts the game. Play continues in a clockwise direction with each player trying to butt one of his own tiles to one end of the line of play. If a player is unable to lay a tile, they signify this by banging a fist (or a tile) on the table. This is called **KNOCKING**.

OBJECT OF THE GAME

The object of the game is to get rid of all your tiles. The game ends when one player achieves this and calls out **"DOMINO"** or when no further play is possible and every player has to knock. The player who calls "domino" wins the game and records their score. They do this by adding up the total number of pips on their opponents' unplayed tiles. In the case of a partnership game, they then subtract the sum of their partner's remaining tiles from this total.

It is possible for a team that has called "domino" to end up losing the game because the other player in a team has a higher pip count than the combined total of the opponents' unplayed tiles.

If a situation arises where no further play is possible, the player with the lowest pip count scores the total of their opponents' tiles. In a partnership game, the two teams compare totals and the team with the lowest pip count scores the difference between the two totals.

SLEEPERS

If four people are playing **BLOCK** and they have decided to remove seven tiles each, there will be no tiles left facedown in the **BONEYARD**. However, if they decide to draw hands of less than seven tiles, there will be some tiles left in the boneyard. These tiles are called **SLEEPERS** and you can try to figure out which tiles they might be.

WINNING STRATEGY

Try to play your highest numbers early in the game in case you get stuck with them at the end of the round, where their high value will count against you. Get rid of your doubles at the first opportunity too, because they are much harder to play. Try to make sure that you are not **BLOCKED** (unable to lay a tile) on your next move and try to ensure that your opponent is!

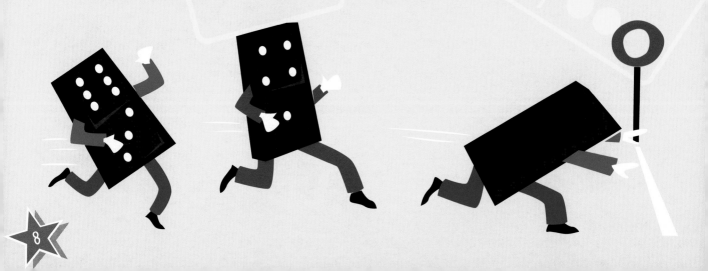

GAME 2: ENDS

 This is a game for four people. The rules are very simple.

If a player (A) doesn't have a matching domino when it is their turn, they have to ask the player on their left (B) for one. Player B must hand it over and player A must lay it down.

If player B doesn't have a matching tile to give to player A, they must ask the player on THEIR left (C) for one. They hand it to the first player (A). They lay it down and now it is the turn of the second person (B) to play.

If the third player (C) doesn't have one either, they must ask the player on their left (D) for one. This is given to the first person (A) to play, and then it is the turn of the next player (B).

If none of the players have a matching domino, player A can now lay down any domino they wish.

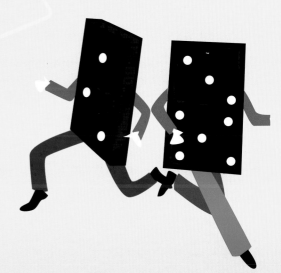

The first player to get rid of all their dominoes wins the game.

GAME 3: MUGGINS

 In some domino games you score points as you go along. The best-known game of this type is called **MUGGINS**.

It is a game for two to four players and is best played as a partnership game. Before the game, all players must agree on whether to draw five, six, or seven tiles. The first player (or team) to reach a score of 61 wins the game.

Each player must try to score as many points as possible while attempting to get rid of all their dominoes.

Points are scored by laying a tile so that the ends of the line of play equal five or multiples of five. One point is scored for each 5 pips.

ONE POINT

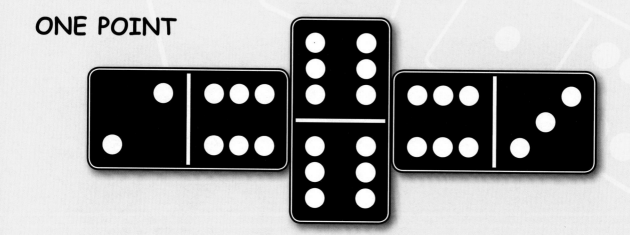

You count ALL the pips on an exposed double. The examples here show typical scores of two, three, and four points.

TWO POINTS

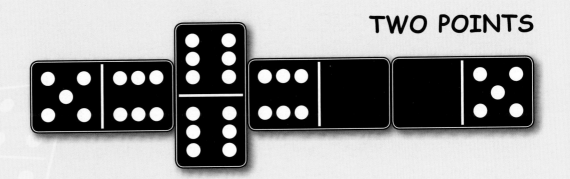

THREE POINTS

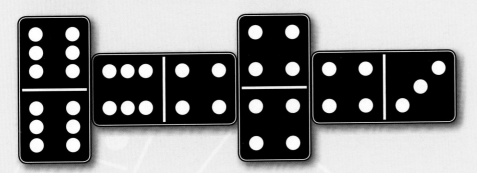

FOUR POINTS

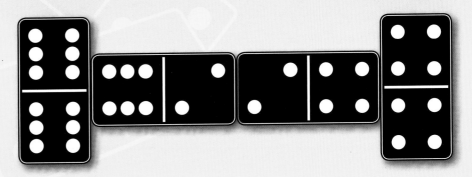

The player with the highest double starts the game, and if it happens to be the double-five, they immediately score two points! A score sheet is kept in order to keep track of the play.

When one player **GOES OUT** (calls "domino") the other players count up the pips on their remaining tiles. The winner scores one point for every five-point difference between the two teams' pips.

Here is an example of scoring in a partnership game. Player A has gone out and his partner (C) has a total of 6 pips left in his hand. The opposing partners (B and D) total up their combined number of pips, let's say 14. Player C's total of 6 is deducted from this (14 − 6), which equals 8. This number is rounded up to the nearest multiple of 5, which in this case is 10. (Remember, one point is scored for each 5 pips). So, Player A and his partner score an extra two points.

WINNING STRATEGY

If you can lay a tile so that the number at each end of the line of play is the same, and you are holding another tile with this number on it, you should do so.

Watch your partner's play very carefully. Are they trying to use this strategy? Help them if you can by trying to place doubles on the tiles that they have played.

GAME 4: FIVES AND THREES

 This game is very similar to **MUGGINS**.
Here you score all multiples of 3 and 5.

Individual players can play it, but it is best as a partnership game.

Each player draws seven tiles and the game starts with the player holding the lowest double. Play continues in the usual way.

Any play that results in the pips at each end of the line of play being a multiple of 3 or 5 scores one point for each of the multiples. The player or partnership that goes out scores one extra point. If you are playing as two teams of partners, each team adds up their score at the end of each round. Then, you subtract the scores to find the difference. The team with the highest score for that round takes these points. The next round begins. The first team to 31 wins.

If you are lucky enough to make the pips at the line of play total 15, you score 8 points! This is because 15 is a multiple of 3 (five points) and 5 (three points).

In this example, A and C are one team, B and D the other. A starts the game with the double-blank.

A1	0-0		B1	0-3	(1 point)
C1	0-6	(3 points)	D1	6-6	(8 points!)

A2	3-6	(6 points)	B2	6-4	
C2	6-5	(3 points)	D2	4-1	(2 points)

A3	1-1		B3	5-5	(4 points)
C3	5-3	(1 point)	D3	3-4	(2 points)

A4	4-4	(2 points)	B4	4-2	
C4	2-2	(2 points)	D4	2-3	(1 point)

A5	3-3		B5	1-0	(2 points)
C5	0-4	(2 points)	D5	4-5	

A6	5-1		B6	1-6	(4 points)
C6	6-2		D6	2-5	

A7	Knocks		B7	Knocks
C7	3-1	(2 points) and is out!		

A & C Total is 22 (21 + 1 for going out).
B & D Total is 24.

So, although A and C went out first, B and D win the round and are awarded two points.

A TYPICAL GAME OF
"FIVES AND THREES"

A, B, and D are left with these tiles

15

GAME 5: DRAW

 This is an interesting variation on **BLOCK**, for two or more players. First, decide on a playing order.

Each player draws five tiles.

The first player can lay down any tile from their hand. It does not have to be a double.

The second player now has three options:

• They can play one of their tiles to the table – matching one of the ends in the normal way, or…

• They can draw another tile from the boneyard and then play to the table, or…

• They can continue picking up tiles from the boneyard. They can stop whenever they feel like it, and the turn ends only when they play a tile to the line of play. They must play a matching tile if they can.

Play now passes to the next player, who has the same three options.

Play continues around the table in this way.

The last two tiles in the boneyard must never be touched. These play no part in the game.

The game continues and the first player to lose all their tiles is the winner. If nobody can go out, the players' pips are added up and the person with the lowest number of pips wins the game.

GAME 6: SEBASTAPOL

This is a game for four players who play as individuals.

The tiles are thoroughly shuffled and each player draws seven.

The player with the double-six lays it down to start the game, and play continues in a clockwise direction.

Tiles must first be laid on all four sides of the double-six, forming a cross.

If a player doesn't have a six, play passes to the next person. Only when the cross has been successfully formed can play continue. You are now allowed to play to any one of the four open arms of the cross.

The scoring is the same as for **BLOCK**.

GAME 7: CYPRUS

 CYPRUS is similar to **SEBASTAPOL**. Once again, it is a game for four players.

Seven tiles each are drawn and the player with the double-six starts the game.

This time ALL the sixes must be laid before play can continue.

A star shape is formed, like this:

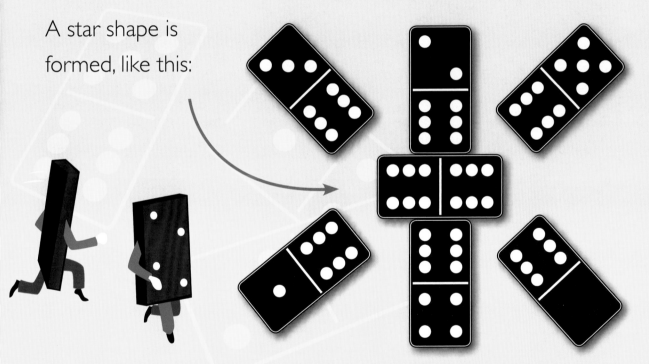

Play now continues and all six wings can be played on. Once again, the first player to lose all their tiles wins the round and scores the total sum of their opponents' pips.

If the game cannot be completed, the pips in the players' hands are totaled and the person with the lowest total scores the sum of the other three players' pips.

GAME 8: SNIFF

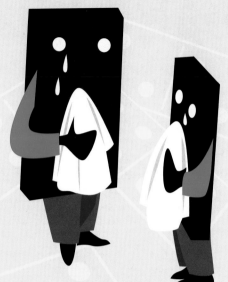

SNIFF could be called "Son of Muggins" because it shares many of the same characteristics. It is a game for two to four players and can be played as a partnership game.

Two players would draw seven dominoes each, three players would each draw six, and four players would draw five tiles each.

As usual, the aim of the game is to lose all your tiles and go out. However, as in Muggins, you can score along the way. If you can play so that the two ends of the line of play add up to five or multiples of five you score points. Unlike Muggins, the line of play in Sniff may have up to four ends – so much higher scores are possible.

Once you have decided on a playing order, the first player can lay any domino that he chooses from his hand and play continues in a clockwise direction. If he can start with one of the five dominoes below, he will immediately begin to score points.

Until the first double is played, the line of play has only two ends. The first double that is laid (it could even be the first tile played) is called the **SNIFF** and is a **SPINNER,** which means that you can play off all sides of it. It can be laid along the line of play or across it, as the player chooses.

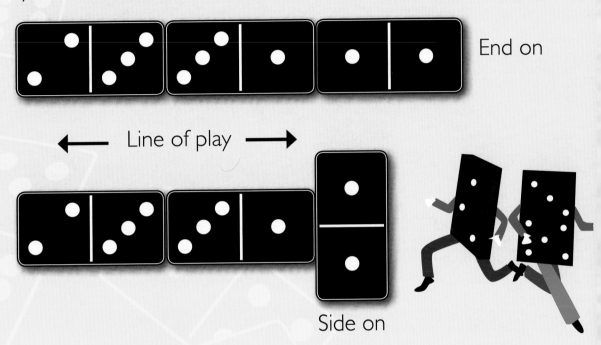

End on

Line of play

Side on

For the next move, you must play off of either of the open ends of a sniff. Once this is done, you may play off the sides. You can either lay the tile end on or side on.

If you play side on, you can play off the other end of the sniff, but only after this move. Any doubles played after the sniff must be played across the line of play and are not spinners. If a player is unable to play, they must draw up to two tiles from the boneyard. If they still can't match a tile, play passes to the next person.

The first person to go out scores the total of his opponents' remaining pips, rounded up to the nearest five points. If no one can go out, the person with the lowest remaining pip count wins the round and scores the total of his opponents' pips rounded up to the nearest five.

The first person to score 250 points is the outright winner. The following illustration shows how a game of sniff might proceed:

THE SNIFF

WINNING STRATEGY

Scoring on the table should be your main aim. If you are unable to make a score, try to play so that the ends of the line of play match numbers that you are holding.

Don't let your opponents know if your play has been forced upon you. The longer the game lasts, the better you should be able to figure out which tiles your opponents are holding. Then you can make your play accordingly.

GAME 9: CONCENTRATION

 This game is suitable for all ages and any number of players. It is similar to the card game Pairs.

HOW TO PLAY

The dominoes are spread out, pip side down, across the table and thoroughly shuffled. Each player takes turns to turn over two dominoes. If the pips on the two dominoes total 12, the player keeps the two dominoes and scores one point. This is called **MAKING A TRICK**. They can now turn over two more dominoes and can continue to do this until they fail to make a total of 12. If the two dominoes do not total 12, the player places them facedown back in the boneyard.

It is now the second player's turn. They may have noticed that one of the previous player's two dominoes would help them to reach 12. If so, they can pick that one up as their second domino to make a trick, if they can remember where it is!

A 5–5 can be matched by finding the 1–1 or 0–2.

The 6–6 can only be matched
with the 0–0.

There are 14 possible tricks and there are 34 different ways to
achieve them. The round ends when all 14 tricks have been made
and there are no more tiles left in the boneyard. The person with
the highest number of tricks wins the round. One point is scored
for each trick. It is usual to play ten rounds, and the person with the
highest number of points is the Grand Champion.

This game is as much about
having a good memory as having
good luck.

The more rounds that are
played, the easier it should
become to remember where
certain dominoes are located.

GAME 10: MATADOR

 This is a game for two to four people, playing as individuals.

Each player draws five, six, or seven tiles. Once again, the winner is the person who gets rid of all their tiles first.

In **MATADOR,** the main aim is to play to the **RULE OF SEVEN**.

Four of the tiles act in the same way as the jokers in a pack of cards. They are **WILD** tiles and may be played at any time. These are the **MATADORS,** which are the three tiles that total 7 plus the double-blank:

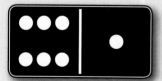 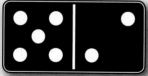 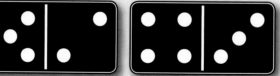 

They can be laid with or against the line of play. Decide upon a playing order.

The first player can lay down any tile from their hand. The next player can only extend the line of play if they can butt a tile to it so that the pips on the two touching half tiles total 7.

All doubles must be played along the line of play and not across it.

A Matador may be played against either end of the line of play, regardless of the number of pips. If it is laid with the line of play, only the exposed end can be played on. If it is laid across the line of play, then the pip count of the half tile laid against it may be added to either half of the Matador tile.

Matadors can be laid against each other!

If you cannot play to the rule of seven, you must draw a tile from the boneyard. You do not have to play a Matador even if you cannot obey the rule of seven. You can choose to draw from the boneyard instead.

When the boneyard is empty, you can call **PASS** even if you still hold a Matador. The round ends when one player loses all their tiles OR all players pass.

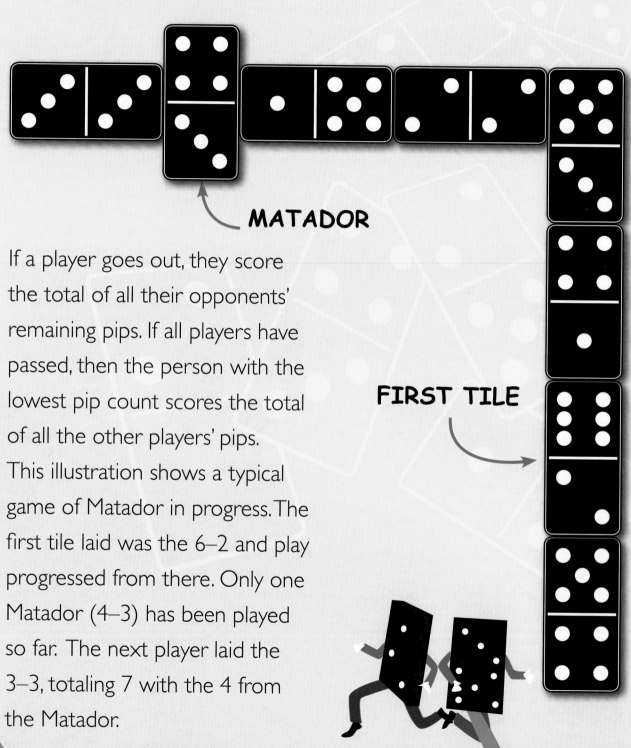

MATADOR

FIRST TILE

If a player goes out, they score the total of all their opponents' remaining pips. If all players have passed, then the person with the lowest pip count scores the total of all the other players' pips. This illustration shows a typical game of Matador in progress. The first tile laid was the 6–2 and play progressed from there. Only one Matador (4–3) has been played so far. The next player laid the 3–3, totaling 7 with the 4 from the Matador.

DOMINO PUZZLES

The following puzzles are for you to solve on your own!

Take these six dominoes: 0–0, 0–1, 0–2, 1–1, 1–2, and 2–2.

Puzzle 1: The challenge is to arrange the six tiles in a square pattern with all the numbers butting correctly. This is the pattern that you must achieve:

Puzzle 2: This puzzle is a bit more difficult and will probably take you a bit longer. The task is to use all 28 tiles and form them into 7 square shapes like this:

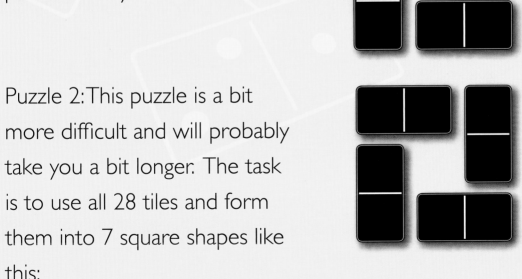

Don't forget that all the butting ends must match!
See page 32 for solutions.

See page 32 for solutions.

MIND-READING DOMINOES

 Here's a magic trick you might like to try out on your friends.

Secretly remove one of the tiles so that there are only 27 tiles in the box. In this example, the 6–1 is taken out. Nobody will ever notice that the box is one short. Write the following message on a piece of paper:

> # I predict that the two numbers on the ends of your game will be a six and a one!

Fold it up and put it in your pocket. Your preparation is complete!

WHAT TO DO

Take the 27 dominoes out of the box and play a game of Block in the usual way. At the end of the game, the two ends of the line of play will ALWAYS match with the one that you have taken; in this case, the 6–1 tile.

Once you have finished your game, ask your opponent to call out the numbers of the pips at each end of the line of play. You can then amaze them by revealing the prediction from your pocket.

THE "MISSING" DOMINO

SOLUTIONS TO PUZZLES

Puzzle 1

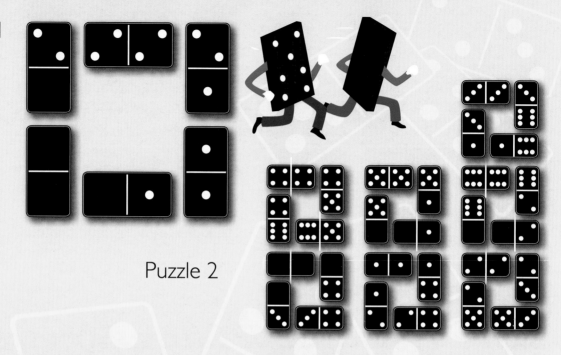

Puzzle 2

Published in 2022 by Windmill Books,
an Imprint of Rosen Publishing
29 East 21st Street, New York, NY 10010

Cataloging-in-Publication Data

Names: Tremaine, Jon.
Title: Dominoes for beginners / Jon Tremaine.
Description: New York : Windmill Books, 2022. | Series: Game on!
Identifiers: ISBN 9781538270172 (pbk.) | ISBN 9781538270196 (library bound) | ISBN 9781538270189 (6 pack) | ISBN 9781538270202 (ebook)
Subjects: LCSH: Dominoes–Juvenile literature.
Classification: LCC GV1467.T75 2022 | DDC 795.3'2–dc23

Manufactured in the United States of America

CPSIA Compliance Information: Batch BSWM22: For Further Information contact Rosen Publishing, New York, New York at 1-800-237-9932